As busy parents of five growing kids, we'i
intentional resources to grow our faith to,
perfect activity to help us interact with Gc   .. Word, ...s how it applies to
our lives, and hide it deep in our hearts. H..,.., ...ia for any family
seeking to grow in Christ!

CHRIS AND JENNI GRAEBE, hosts of *The Rhythm of Us* podcast

As a mom of six, I work hard to teach our children about Jesus and
the importance of knowing God's Word. But if I'm being really honest,
our kids often put Scripture memorization in the same category as
homework and chores. The *Topical Memory System for Kids*, though, turns
grumbling into game playing. I wish I'd had this when I was growing up!
(But guess what, grown-ups? We get to play it too!)

TERESA SWANSTROM ANDERSON, author of the Get Wisdom
Bible Studies

TMS for Kids comes with many foundational verses, and it allows room
for quality family time to turn into a fun period of Scripture memory. The
checklist, the verses, and the review all remind me of *TMS*, but with the
bonus of easy, pass-along cards for younger children.

OSAZE MURRAY, director of training for The Navigators'
Train, Develop, Care

Memorizing Scripture is a key habit in developing a deep and intimate
relationship with God. A believer without Scripture memory is like
a doctor without a stethoscope. *TMS for Kids* is a great way to equip
children—early on—for writing God's Word on their hearts. Memorizing
Scripture builds an operating system for young minds to view the world
through God's eyes rather than their own. Kids love games, and the
pairing of playing with memorizing Scripture is the perfect combination
for parents and grandparents to get the kids in their lives exposed to the
Bible.

BEN NUGENT, US Collegiate Director, AND MELISSA NUGENT,
US Collegiate Staff Placement Director at The Navigators

Topical Memory System for KiDS

Be like Jesus!

HIDE GOD'S WORD IN YOUR HEART

NavPress

A NavPress resource published in alliance with Tyndale House Publishers

NavPress ◣

NavPress is the publishing ministry of The Navigators, an international Christian organization and leader in personal spiritual development. NavPress is committed to helping people grow spiritually and enjoy lives of meaning and hope through personal and group resources that are biblically rooted, culturally relevant, and highly practical.

For more information, visit NavPress.com.

The Team:
David Zimmerman, Publisher and Acquisitions Editor; Elizabeth Schroll, Copy Editor; Olivia Eldredge, Operations Manager; Sarah Susan Richardson, Designer; Sarah K. Johnson, Proofreader

For information about special discounts for bulk purchases, please contact Tyndale House Publishers at csresponse@tyndale.com, or call 1-855-277-9400.

ISBN 978-1-64158-550-7

Printed in China

29	28	27	26	25	24	23
7	6	5	4	3	2	1

Contents

Begin a Lifetime of Scripture Memory and Meditation

You and your child can memorize Scripture. It's fun, it's easier than you think, and it's a tried-and-true way of growing in the assurance that God claims you as his and wants to include you in his world-saving work.

Scripture memory is a great practice to instill in a young person at an early age. Children's minds are primed for absorbing and internalizing information. They enjoy repetition, which is an essential ingredient in the Scripture-memorization process. And Scripture memory is best done with others—we recite what we remember to people we love and trust, and they help us keep moving forward. All the while, the practice of memorizing Scripture, not just the memorized verses, becomes internalized and normalized for your child. They're learning a skill that will help them for a lifetime.

Attitude makes the difference. Because the Bible was written thousands of years ago and was not written specifically for children, your child will encounter unfamiliar and stretching words along the way. (We've included a kid-friendly glossary in the back of the book.) Encourage your child. Express delight in them and their desire to memorize God's Word. Celebrate with them when a particular verse is especially meaningful to them. You can count on God's help as you memorize together. Remember his wisdom—"These commandments that I give you today are to be on your hearts" (Deuteronomy 6:6, NIV) and "Let the Word of Christ—the Message—have the run of the house" (Colossians 3:16, MSG).

The *Topical Memory System* has been helping people memorize Scripture for decades, and it will help you and your kids too! The tried-and-true methods of *TMS* are the foundation of this fun game. This is the second volume of the *Topical Memory System for Kids*: The first volume features series A, B, and C of the memory verses from the *Topical Memory System*; *Be like Jesus!* features series D and E.

What Scripture Memory Will Do for Your Child

Memorizing and meditating on God's Word helps you overcome worry. You can experience God's perfect peace by knowing his promises and having them written on your heart.

Another benefit is victory over sin. The psalmist wrote, "I have hidden your word in my heart that I might not sin against you" (Psalm 119:11, NIV). God's Word hidden in your heart is the sword of the Spirit, available for battle at any time against sin and Satan.

These things are true even for very young children. Apprehension about making friends, a new start at school—these things can be unsettling and cause much anxiety. God's precious Word will remind your child of his promises and of his care and desire to help him or her overcome worry, sin, or any other obstacle that a young child might encounter.

Scripture memory will also help a child gain confidence in talking about Jesus. It may be the very first time that they begin to think of witnessing or evangelism. How lovely to start this desire to share the Good News when full of enthusiasm and the energy of youth!

Finally, Scripture memory will help your child (and you!) keep spiritually fit. You will both experience immediate benefits and become better equipped to meet future needs and opportunities.

How to PLAY

The *Topical Memory System for Kids: Be like Jesus!* contains 24 verses in the New International Version (NIV) and *The Message* (MSG). The verses are printed on perforated sheets. Tear out the cards for the version of your choice.

Shuffle the cards and spread them out in rows with the verses faceup.

The first player selects two cards and reads them out loud, turning each card over once it's been read. If the cards are a match, the player reads the topic and the reference. The player keeps the cards, and the next player takes a turn.

If the two cards don't match, the player turns the cards back over, and it is the next player's turn.

The game ends when all the cards have been matched. The player with the most matches wins.

NOTE: For younger children, the game can be played with fewer cards. Play with 8 verses at first (16 cards), then work your way up to 16 (32 cards), and then finally play using all 24 verses (48 cards).

Next-Level Game Play

As your kids memorize these passages, try using the cards as flash cards. The first player looks at the back of the card and reads the topic and reference out loud. The second player follows along as the first player recites the verse from memory. The player keeps each card he or she gets right. The memorization has to be word-perfect! The player with the most cards at the end wins.

Your kids can also combine this deck with other decks in the Topical Memory System for Kids series. So you can expand the matching game to 36, 48, and even 60 verses (120 cards)!

Between Games

Your kids will get better and better at the game if they practice. The proven method for memorizing Scripture from the *Topical Memory System* can be used in between games.

Each verse in *TMS for Kids* is part of a series. The topics help you understand the meaning of the verses. They also give you mental "hooks" with which to draw a particular verse from memory when you need it. They serve as pegs on which to hang the verses as you learn them.

Topics are printed on the back of each card, along with the Scripture reference for the passage.

Knowing the reference for each verse you memorize makes it possible to find the verses in the Bible immediately when you need them for personal use or in helping others. So make the reference a part of each verse you memorize.

The surest way to remember the reference is to say it both before and after the verse each time you review it. This will connect the reference and the verse in your mind. This may seem tedious at first, but it is important—and it works!

So then, using these cards:

- Start by looking at the back of card 1. Read the topic, then the reference.

- Flip card 1 over and read the first half of the passage.

- Now read the second half of the passage from card 2.

- Flip card 2 over and read the reference, then the topic.

Remember that the goal is to memorize the verses, so encourage your kids to do so, gradually reciting the passage from memory and using the cards to check their progress. It's good to focus on two verses at a time for a week at a time. Included in this book are questions you and your child can talk about as they memorize these verses.

Once a verse is memorized, it's helpful to review it every now and then. The game is a good way of doing this!

Checklist:
The Topical Memory System for Kids:
Be like Jesus!

Place a check next to the reference of the verses your child has successfully memorized.

Follow Jesus

○ *Put Jesus First!* ___Matthew 6:33 ___Luke 9:23

○ *Be Different like Jesus!* ___1 John 2:15-16 ___Romans 12:2

○ *Hold Tight to Jesus!* ___1 Corinthians 15:58 ___Hebrews 12:3

○ *Serve Others!* ___Mark 10:45 ___2 Corinthians 4:5

○ *Share!* ___Proverbs 3:9-10 ___2 Corinthians 9:6-7

○ *Love the Whole World!* ___Acts 1:8 ___Matthew 28:19-20

Live like Jesus

○ *Love!* ___John 13:34-35 ___1 John 3:18

○ *Be Humble!* ___Philippians 2:3-4 ___1 Peter 5:5-6

○ *Be Pure!* ___1 John 3:3 ___1 Peter 2:11

○ *Tell the Truth!* ___Leviticus 19:11 ___Acts 24:16

○ *Trust God!* ___Hebrews 11:6 ___Romans 4:20-21

○ *Do Your Best!* ___Galatians 6:9-10 ___Matthew 5:16

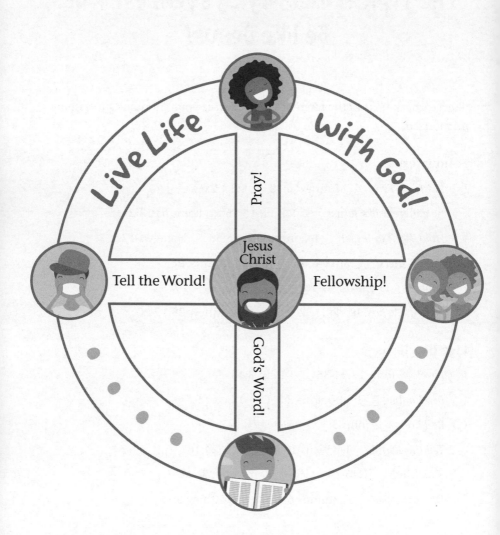

Adapted from The Wheel Illustration. Used by permission of The Navigators. All rights reserved.

Follow Jesus

Jesus died on a cross to save people like you and me! That was an amazing thing he did. But he did even more than that! Jesus invited people like you and me to follow him, and to invite others to follow him too. And when they did, they changed the world!

Jesus wasn't just looking for people to follow him around. He wanted them to live the way he lived and to love the way he loved. He wanted people to be different because they followed him. People like you and me, more and more like him!

Week 1
Put Jesus First!

> But seek first his kingdom and his righteousness, and all these things will be given to you as well.
>
> Matthew 6:33, NIV

> Steep your life in God-reality, God-initiative, God-provisions. Don't worry about missing out. You'll find all your everyday human concerns will be met.
>
> Matthew 6:33, MSG

Read Matthew 6:25-34 together to see the verse in context. Then read the verse off the cards.

- Start by looking at the back of card 1. Read the topic, then the reference.
- Flip card 1 over and read the first half of the passage.
- Now read the second half of the passage from card 2.
- Flip card 2 over and read the reference, then the topic.

Some questions for you and your child to discuss:

- What do you picture when you hear the word *kingdom*? What does that tell you about who Jesus is?
- What does it mean to "seek righteousness"? If Jesus is good, and he wants us to be good, how do we learn how to be good?
- When was the last time you worried about something? What were you worried about? Why don't we need to worry about things when we put Jesus first?

> Then he said to them all: "Whoever wants to be my disciple must deny themselves and take up their cross daily and follow me."
>
> Luke 9:23, NIV

> Then he told them what they could expect for themselves: "Anyone who intends to come with me has to let me lead. You're not in the driver's seat—I am. Don't run from suffering; embrace it. Follow me and I'll show you how."
>
> Luke 9:23, MSG

Read Luke 9:18-27 together to see the verse in context. Then read the verse off the cards using the process on the previous page.

Some questions for you and your child to discuss:

- What got in the way of you following Jesus this past week?
- What does it mean to let Jesus lead you?
- Putting Jesus first means putting him before you. How can you do that tomorrow?

Pray with your child about trusting Jesus enough to let him lead.

Follow Jesus:
Put Jesus First!

Week 2
Be Different like Jesus!

Do not love the world or anything in the world. If anyone loves the world, love for the Father is not in them. For everything in the world—the lust of the flesh, the lust of the eyes, and the pride of life—comes not from the Father but from the world.

1 John 2:15-16, NIV

Don't love the world's ways. Don't love the world's goods. Love of the world squeezes out love for the Father. Practically everything that goes on in the world—wanting your own way, wanting everything for yourself, wanting to appear important—has nothing to do with the Father. It just isolates you from him.

1 John 2:15-16, MSG

Read 1 John 2:12-17 together to see the verses in context. Then read the verses off the cards.

- Start by looking at the back of card 1. Read the topic, then the reference.
- Flip card 1 over and read the first half of the passage.
- Now read the second half of the passage from card 2.
- Flip card 2 over and read the reference, then the topic.

Some questions for you and your child to discuss:

- What made it hard for you to love God this week? What squeezed in between you and God?
- Why would "wanting your own way, wanting everything for yourself, wanting to appear important" make it harder to love God?
- Even though we shouldn't love the world's ways or the world's goods, God loves the world (see John 3:16). So how should we treat the world?

> Do not conform to the pattern of this world, but be transformed by the renewing of your mind. Then you will be able to test and approve what God's will is—his good, pleasing and perfect will.
>
> Romans 12:2, NIV

> Don't become so well-adjusted to your culture that you fit into it without even thinking. Instead, fix your attention on God. You'll be changed from the inside out. Readily recognize what he wants from you, and quickly respond to it. Unlike the culture around you, always dragging you down to its level of immaturity, God brings the best out of you, develops well-formed maturity in you.
>
> Romans 12:2, MSG

Read Romans 11:32–12:2 together to see the verse in context. Then read the verse off the cards using the process on the previous page.

Some questions for you and your child to discuss:

- How do you fix your attention on God?

- When you hear about "the renewing of your mind," what do you picture God doing? Why?

- If God brings out the best in you tomorrow, what do you think might happen?

Pray with your child about resisting temptation to be more like the world than like Jesus.

Week 3
Hold Tight to Jesus!

Therefore, my dear brothers and sisters, stand firm. Let nothing move you. Always give yourselves fully to the work of the Lord, because you know that your labor in the Lord is not in vain.

1 Corinthians 15:58, NIV

With all this going for us, my dear, dear friends, stand your ground. And don't hold back. Throw yourselves into the work of the Master, confident that nothing you do for him is a waste of time or effort.

1 Corinthians 15:58, MSG

Read 1 Corinthians 15:50-58 together to see the verse in context. Then read the verse off the cards.

- Start by looking at the back of card 1. Read the topic, then the reference.
- Flip card 1 over and read the first half of the passage.
- Now read the second half of the passage from card 2.
- Flip card 2 over and read the reference, then the topic.

Some questions for you and your child to discuss:

- What does it look like to give yourself to Jesus?
- When have you been embarrassed to follow Jesus?
- What helps you keep following him even when you're embarrassed?

> Consider him who endured such opposition from sinners, so that you will not grow weary and lose heart.
>
> Hebrews 12:3, NIV

> When you find yourselves flagging in your faith, go over that story again, item by item, that long litany of hostility he plowed through. *That* will shoot adrenaline into your souls!
>
> Hebrews 12:3, MSG

Read Hebrews 12:1-13 together to see the verse in context. Then read the verse off the cards using the process on the previous page.

Some questions for you and your child to discuss:

- Why do you think people chose not to follow Jesus?
- How do you think Jesus responded to people who chose not to follow him?
- What do you say to Jesus when you're feeling sad or lonely?

Pray with your child about being faithful to Jesus even when it's uncomfortable to do so.

Week 4
Serve Others!

For even the Son of Man did not come to be served, but to serve, and to give his life as a ransom for many.

Mark 10:45, NIV

That is what the Son of Man has done: He came to serve, not to be served—and then to give away his life in exchange for many who are held hostage.

Mark 10:45, MSG

Read Mark 10:35-45 together to see the verse in context. Then read the verse off the cards.

- Start by looking at the back of card 1. Read the topic, then the reference.
- Flip card 1 over and read the first half of the passage.
- Now read the second half of the passage from card 2.
- Flip card 2 over and read the reference, then the topic.

Some questions for you and your child to discuss:

- Who is speaking these words?
- What is the difference between serving and being served?
- What does it mean to give away your life?

For what we preach is not ourselves, but Jesus Christ as Lord, and ourselves as your servants for Jesus' sake.

2 Corinthians 4:5, NIV

Remember, our Message is not about ourselves; we're proclaiming Jesus Christ, the Master. All we are is messengers, errand runners from Jesus for you.

2 Corinthians 4:5, MSG

Read 2 Corinthians 4:1-18 together to see the verse in context. Then read the verse off the cards using the process on the previous page.

Some questions for you and your child to discuss:

- How can you be a messenger for Jesus?
- What's the difference between preaching ourselves and proclaiming Jesus as Lord?
- How does it feel to think of yourself as a servant?

Pray with your child, asking God for opportunities to serve him and other people.

Follow Jesus:
Serve Others!

Week 5
Share!

> Honor the LORD with your wealth,
>   with the firstfruits of all your crops;
> then your barns will be filled to overflowing,
>   and your vats will brim over with new wine.
>
> Proverbs 3:9-10, NIV
>
> Honor GOD with everything you own;
>   give him the first and the best.
> Your barns will burst,
>   your wine vats will brim over.
>
> Proverbs 3:9-10, MSG

Read Proverbs 3:1-12 together to see the verses in context. Then read the verses off the cards.

- Start by looking at the back of card 1. Read the topic, then the reference.

- Flip card 1 over and read the first half of the passage.

- Now read the second half of the passage from card 2.

- Flip card 2 over and read the reference, then the topic.

Some questions for you and your child to discuss:

- When you think of everything you have, what would you say is "the first and the best"?

- Do you think your family is wealthy? Why or why not?

- What does it mean to be "filled to overflowing"?

> Remember this: Whoever sows sparingly will also reap sparingly, and whoever sows generously will also reap generously. Each of you should give what you have decided in your heart to give, not reluctantly or under compulsion, for God loves a cheerful giver.
>
> 2 Corinthians 9:6-7, NIV

> Remember: A stingy planter gets a stingy crop; a lavish planter gets a lavish crop. I want each of you to take plenty of time to think it over, and make up your own mind what you will give. That will protect you against sob stories and arm-twisting. God loves it when the giver delights in the giving.
>
> 2 Corinthians 9:6-7, MSG

Read 2 Corinthians 9:6-15 together to see the verses in context. Then read the verses off the cards using the process on the previous page.

Some questions for you and your child to discuss:

- When was the last time you felt cheerful or delighted? What made you feel that way?
- When was the last time you were especially generous? What made you want to be so generous?
- Why is it good to make up your mind in advance how generous you're willing to be?

Pray with your child, thanking God for his generosity to your family and asking him to help your family be generous to others.

Week 6
Love the Whole World!

> But you will receive power when the Holy Spirit comes on you; and you will be my witnesses in Jerusalem, and in all Judea and Samaria, and to the ends of the earth.
>
> Acts 1:8, NIV

> What you'll get is the Holy Spirit. And when the Holy Spirit comes on you, you will be able to be my witnesses in Jerusalem, all over Judea and Samaria, even to the ends of the world.
>
> Acts 1:8, MSG

Read Acts 1:1-11 together to see the verse in context. Then read the verse off the cards.

- Start by looking at the back of card 1. Read the topic, then the reference.
- Flip card 1 over and read the first half of the passage.
- Now read the second half of the passage from card 2.
- Flip card 2 over and read the reference, then the topic.

Some questions for you and your child to discuss:

- What does it mean to be Jesus' "witness"?
- When was the last time you felt powerful? How did it feel? What did you do?
- What do you think of when you think of the Holy Spirit?

> Therefore go and make disciples of all nations, baptizing them in the name of the Father and of the Son and of the Holy Spirit, and teaching them to obey everything I have commanded you. And surely I am with you always, to the very end of the age.
>
> Matthew 28:19-20, NIV
>
> Go out and train everyone you meet, far and near, in this way of life, marking them by baptism in the threefold name: Father, Son, and Holy Spirit. Then instruct them in the practice of all I have commanded you. I'll be with you as you do this, day after day after day, right up to the end of the age.
>
> Matthew 28:19-20, MSG

Read Matthew 28:16-20 together to see the verses in context. Then read the verses off the cards using the process on the previous page.

Some questions for you and your child to discuss:

- What does "make disciples" mean to you?
- Who first told you the good news about Jesus?
- Who can you tell the good news about Jesus to this week?

Pray with your child that God will make you bold as you share the gospel.

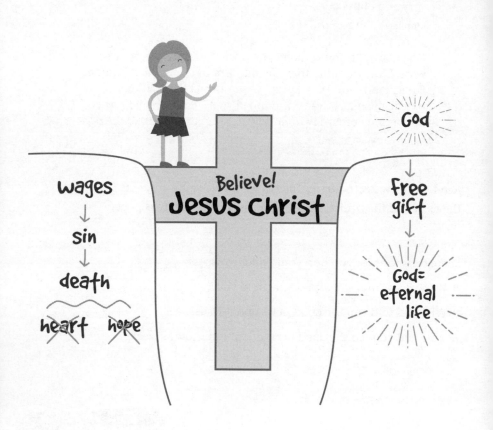

Live like Jesus

Having Jesus Christ in our lives makes us different. People notice! And they are drawn to the difference between how our lives look and how the world looks. God is glorified through the way we live!

God's goal for each of us is that we become increasingly like Jesus. We feel pressure, though, to become increasingly like the world and believe its wrong assumptions about what life should look like. Not only pressure, though—we're also tempted to follow the world's path to success, which often takes us in a different direction from the way God is going.

When we look just like the world, it becomes harder for our families and friends to see Jesus through us.

But good news—God helps us become more like Jesus! Through the Holy Spirit and through God's Word (which we're memorizing!), our instincts are trained in the direction of Jesus.

The bridge illustration is often used to show how believing in Jesus moves us from death to life. But it also shows us how God is leading us in a life-giving direction. This goes on our whole lives! And that path always leads us into life with Jesus.

Week 7
Love!

A new command I give you: Love one another. As I have loved you, so you must love one another. By this everyone will know that you are my disciples, if you love one another.

John 13:34-35, NIV

Let me give you a new command: Love one another. In the same way I loved you, you love one another. This is how everyone will recognize that you are my disciples—when they see the love you have for each other.

John 13:34-35, MSG

Read John 13:31-38 together to see the verses in context. Then read the verses off the cards.

- Start by looking at the back of card 1. Read the topic, then the reference.
- Flip card 1 over and read the first half of the passage.
- Now read the second half of the passage from card 2.
- Flip card 2 over and read the reference, then the topic.

Some questions for you and your child to discuss:

- Whom do you love? How do you show your love for them?
- How has Jesus shown love to you?
- Whom can you show love to tomorrow?

> Dear children, let us not love with words or speech but with actions and in truth.
>
> 1 John 3:18, NIV
>
> My dear children, let's not just talk about love; let's practice real love.
>
> 1 John 3:18, MSG

Read 1 John 3:11-24 together to see the verse in context. Then read the verse off the cards using the process on the previous page.

Some questions for you and your child to discuss:

- What does practicing real love look like?
- How do you love people with words? How do you love people with actions?
- How can you practice loving tomorrow?

Live like Jesus: Love!

Pray with your child, asking God to help you love more consistently and practically.

Week 8
Be Humble!

Do nothing out of selfish ambition or vain conceit. Rather, in humility value others above yourselves, not looking to your own interests but each of you to the interests of the others.

Philippians 2:3-4, NIV

Don't push your way to the front; don't sweet-talk your way to the top. Put yourself aside, and help others get ahead. Don't be obsessed with getting your own advantage. Forget yourselves long enough to lend a helping hand.

Philippians 2:3-4, MSG

Read Philippians 2:1-11 together to see the verses in context. Then read the verses off the cards.

- Start by looking at the back of card 1. Read the topic, then the reference.
- Flip card 1 over and read the first half of the passage.
- Now read the second half of the passage from card 2.
- Flip card 2 over and read the reference, then the topic.

Some questions for you and your child to discuss:

- What does being selfish look like?
- When was the last time you pushed your way to the front? What happened?
- How can you help others get ahead tomorrow?

In the same way, you who are younger, submit yourselves to your elders. All of you, clothe yourselves with humility toward one another, because,

> "God opposes the proud
> but shows favor to the humble."

Humble yourselves, therefore, under God's mighty hand, that he may lift you up in due time.

1 Peter 5:5-6, NIV

And you who are younger must follow your leaders. But all of you, leaders and followers alike, are to be down to earth with each other, for—

> God has had it with the proud,
> But takes delight in just plain people.

So be content with who you are, and don't put on airs. God's strong hand is on you; he'll promote you at the right time.

1 Peter 5:5-6, MSG

Read 1 Peter 5:1-11 together to see the verses in context. Then read the verses off the cards using the process on the previous page.

Some questions for you and your child to discuss:

- How would you describe yourself to someone? What does it mean to be content with who you are?

- What does humbling yourself look like?

- Who are the leaders in your life? How can you follow them this week?

Pray with your child, asking God to make you content with who you are, humble in your relationships, and devoted increasingly to him as your leader.

Live like Jesus:
Be Humble!

Week 9
Be Pure!

All who have this hope in him purify themselves, just as he is pure.

1 John 3:3, NIV

All of us who look forward to his Coming stay ready, with the glistening purity of Jesus' life as a model for our own.

1 John 3:3, MSG

Read 1 John 3:1-6 together to see the verse in context.[1] Then read the verse off the cards.

- Start by looking at the back of card 1. Read the topic, then the reference.
- Flip card 1 over and read the first half of the passage.
- Now read the second half of the passage from card 2.
- Flip card 2 over and read the reference, then the topic.

Some questions for you and your child to discuss:

- What does it mean to be pure?
- What are some ways we might purify ourselves?
- In what ways can Jesus' life be a model for your life?

> Dear friends, I urge you, as foreigners and exiles, to abstain from sinful desires, which wage war against your soul.
>
> 1 Peter 2:11, NIV
>
> Friends, this world is not your home, so don't make yourselves cozy in it. Don't indulge your ego at the expense of your soul.
>
> 1 Peter 2:11, MSG

Read 1 Peter 2:9-12 together to see the verse in context. Then read the verse off the cards using the process on the previous page.

Some questions for you and your child to discuss:

- If "this world is not your home," where do you think God has made a home for you?

- When was the last time you were good and cozy? What did it take for you to move from that cozy spot?

- How can the way you act around your friends give God glory?

[1] In the *Topical Memory System*, on which the *Topical Memory System for Kids* is based, this week's first memory verse is Ephesians 5:3. For this resource, we've selected a more kid-friendly memory verse on the subject of purity.

Pray with your child, asking God to help you both remain pure and resist temptations toward behavior that dishonors God.

21

Week 10
Tell the Truth!

Do not steal.
Do not lie.
Do not deceive one another.
Leviticus 19:11, NIV

Don't steal.
Don't lie.
Don't deceive anyone.
Leviticus 19:11, MSG

Read Leviticus 19:11-14 together to see the verse in context. Then read the verse off the cards.

- Start by looking at the back of card 1. Read the topic, then the reference.
- Flip card 1 over and read the first half of the passage.
- Now read the second half of the passage from card 2.
- Flip card 2 over and read the reference, then the topic.

Some questions for you and your child to discuss:

- What is stealing? Why shouldn't we do it?
- What is lying? Why shouldn't we do it?
- What is deceiving people? Why shouldn't we do it?

> So I strive always to keep my conscience clear before God and man.
>
> Acts 24:16, NIV

> Believe me, I do my level best to keep a clear conscience before God and my neighbors in everything I do.
>
> Acts 24:16, MSG

Read Acts 24:14-16 together to see the verse in context. Then read the verse off the cards using the process on the previous page.

Some questions for you and your child to discuss:

- What is your conscience? How do you know it's there?
- Why should you be honest with your neighbors?
- What makes it hard to be honest with other people? With God?

Pray with your child, thanking God for helping you be truthful and honest with him and with everyone.

Live like Jesus:
Tell the Truth!

Week 11
Trust God!

And without faith it is impossible to please God, because anyone who comes to him must believe that he exists and that he rewards those who earnestly seek him.

Hebrews 11:6, NIV

It's impossible to please God apart from faith. And why? Because anyone who wants to approach God must believe both that he exists *and* that he cares enough to respond to those who seek him.

Hebrews 11:6, MSG

Read Hebrews 11:1-7 together to see the verse in context. Then read the verse off the cards.

- Start by looking at the back of card 1. Read the topic, then the reference.
- Flip card 1 over and read the first half of the passage.
- Now read the second half of the passage from card 2.
- Flip card 2 over and read the reference, then the topic.

Some questions for you and your child to discuss:

- What does it mean to believe?
- How does God take care of you?
- How do you seek God?

> Yet he did not waver through unbelief regarding the promise of God, but was strengthened in his faith and gave glory to God, being fully persuaded that God had power to do what he had promised.
>
> Romans 4:20-21, NIV
>
> He didn't tiptoe around God's promise asking cautiously skeptical questions. He plunged into the promise and came up strong, ready for God, sure that God would make good on what he had said.
>
> Romans 4:20-21, MSG

Read Romans 4:16-25 together to see the verses in context. Then read the verses off the cards using the process on the previous page.

Some questions for you and your child to discuss:

- When have you felt strong in your faith in God?

- In what ways is God powerful in your life?

- What promises from God are important to you?

Pray with your child, thanking God for being someone you can trust.

Week 12
Do Your Best!

> Let us not become weary in doing good, for at the proper time we will reap a harvest if we do not give up. Therefore, as we have opportunity, let us do good to all people, especially to those who belong to the family of believers.
>
> Galatians 6:9-10, NIV
>
> So let's not allow ourselves to get fatigued doing good. At the right time we will harvest a good crop if we don't give up, or quit. Right now, therefore, every time we get the chance, let us work for the benefit of all, starting with the people closest to us in the community of faith.
>
> Galatians 6:9-10, MSG

Read Galatians 6:7-10 together to see the verses in context. Then read the verses off the cards.

- Start by looking at the back of card 1. Read the topic, then the reference.

- Flip card 1 over and read the first half of the passage.

- Now read the second half of the passage from card 2.

- Flip card 2 over and read the reference, then the topic.

Some questions for you and your child to discuss:

- Does doing good ever wear you out? Why?

- What makes you want to quit doing something? Do you get tired or bored or frustrated? What keeps you going?

- When was the last time you had an opportunity to do something nice for someone? What did you do?

> In the same way, let your light shine before others, that they may see your good deeds and glorify your Father in heaven.
>
> Matthew 5:16, NIV

> Now that I've put you there on a hilltop, on a light stand—shine! Keep open house; be generous with your lives. By opening up to others, you'll prompt people to open up with God, this generous Father in heaven.
>
> Matthew 5:16, MSG

Read Matthew 5:13-16 together to see the verse in context. Then read the verse off the cards using the process on the previous page.

Some questions for you and your child to discuss:

- What are you doing when you shine the brightest? Why?
- How can you open up your life to the people around you?
- What is it about God that is generous?

Pray with your child, thanking God that he has made you to shine and gives you people to point to him.

Glossary

Some words in the Bible are hard for kids. Here are some simple definitions of some of the words they might struggle with.

abstain—Do not use. We abstain from something when we have the opportunity to use it (or do it) but choose not to. We abstain from bad things—from lying, for example. We also sometimes abstain from good things! We do this when not using or doing something helps us to spend more time with God or do something God might want us to do. For example, we might abstain from going on a bike ride because we want to work on memorizing a Bible verse.

Bible—God's Book. See "God's Word."

disciple—A follower of Jesus. Disciples are students—but not the kind who sit in a classroom. Disciples of Jesus learn from other disciples of Jesus, like pastors and parents. But disciples also learn by doing—by telling friends about Jesus, by being kind and helpful to neighbors, by praying and reading the Bible.

faith—Making choices that are based on trust. When we trust God enough to do what he tells us, we are showing faith. God gives us faith so we can join in on what he's doing in our lives!

firstfruits—The best part, the first part. In the Bible, people often gave God the firstfruits of the good things that came to them. If they were farmers and grew corn, they would take the first few heads of corn to the Temple as a gift to God. If they had cows and the cows had babies (calves), they would bring the firstborn calf to the Temple. They did this because they knew that anything they had came from God, and giving back to God was a way of thanking him.

glorify—Make famous. When we glorify someone, we tell people about them—not just who they are but also why we love them. In the Bible, people glorify God as a way of reminding themselves and everyone else that God is great!

God's Word—The Bible. The Bible is God's Word to his people. Human beings wrote the books of the Bible, but they were inspired by God to write them. (Sometimes in the Bible, Jesus is called "the Word" because he has shown the world who God is.)

gospel—Good news. When we share the gospel, we are telling people the good news that God loves them and sent Jesus to save them from a life without God, now and forever. (The Bible calls the four stories about Jesus' life "the Gospels.") See "witnessing."

hostility—Anger that hurts someone. It's normal to get angry! Sometimes, though, when we're angry, we hurt people. Sometimes we hurt them on purpose, sometimes accidentally. Anger is normal, but anger is also dangerous!

humble, humility—Comfortable with yourself and not too impressed with yourself. Humility is actually a gift: God promises to lift us up when we don't try to lift ourselves up at the expense of others. God also encourages us to not tear ourselves down: Jesus once told his followers, "You are worth more than many sparrows" (Matthew 10:31, NIV)!

Jesus' Coming—The return of Jesus. There was a time when Jesus was walking the earth, and then he went to heaven. But he promised he would come back for us! When we follow Jesus today, we don't follow him around as he walks the earth but rather spend our time doing things we believe he wants us to do, and we expect to see him any day now!

Kingdom of God—Life as God wants it for us. When we talk about God's Kingdom, we are talking about all the things that are important to God—faith, hope, love, justice, kindness, and more—being important to everyone.

lust—Wanting things in ways that hurt people. It's normal to want things! Sometimes, though, when we want things, we hurt people to get what we want. Sometimes we hurt ourselves. Desire is normal, but lust is desire that is dangerous!

man, mankind—Everyone, all human beings. Sometimes the Bible uses "man" or "mankind" as an easy way of talking about all of us as one big group.

prayer—Talking to God. We pray when we tell God what's going on in our lives, when we ask God questions, when we ask God to help us, and when we thank God for how he's helped us.

righteousness—Being and doing good. Righteousness is when our behaviors and our attitudes are what God wants them to be. Righteous people make the world better!

sin—The opposite of God's best. When we sin, we do or think things that God doesn't want for us. Sin is any action or thought that is the opposite of God's best for our lives.

sow/reap—Plant something/pick something you've planted. Jesus knew a lot of farmers! So he often used words that meant something to farmers. When you make a choice ("sow"), you will have to deal with what that choice makes happen ("reap").

witnessing—Telling other people about Jesus. When we witness, we let people know that God loves them and wants them to have a wonderful life and live with him forever, which is possible because Jesus died for them.

the world—Everyone God made and all the ways that human beings have adapted (and corrupted) God's creation. When we talk about "the world," we mean a lot of things! God loves the world, and yet in many ways the world tends to resist what God wants. So we want to love the world too, but we want to choose the ways of God over the ways of the world. It's actually good for the world when we do.

LEARN TO HIDE GOD'S WORD IN YOUR HEART!

Developed by The Navigators, the *Topical Memory System* kit will improve your knowledge and retention of the Bible, deepen your walk with God, and help you memorize verses that will carry you through the ups and downs in your life.

Kit includes:

- 60 verse cards in ESV, KJV, MSG, NASB, NIV, NKJV, NLT, and NRSV

- Course workbook

- Verse card holder

Wherever books are sold or online at NavPress.com

NavPress is the book-publishing arm of The Navigators.

Since 1933, The Navigators has helped people around the world bring hope and purpose to others in college campuses, local churches, workplaces, neighborhoods, and hard-to-reach places all over the world, face-to-face and person-by-person in an approach we call Life-to-Life® discipleship. We have committed together to know Christ, make Him known, and help others do the same.®

Would you like to join this adventure of discipleship and disciplemaking?

- Take a Digital Discipleship Journey at **navigators.org/disciplemaking**.
- Get more discipleship and disciplemaking content at **thedisciplemaker.org**.
- Find your next book, Bible, or discipleship resource at **navpress.com**.

@NavPressPublishing

@NavPress

@navpressbooks

Steep your life in God-reality, God-initiative, God-provisions.

Don't worry about missing out. You'll find all your everyday human concerns will be met.

Then he told them what they could expect for themselves: "Anyone who intends to come with me has to let me lead."

"You're not in the driver's seat—I am. Don't run from suffering; embrace it. Follow me and I'll show you how."

Follow Jesus:

Put Jesus First!

Matthew 6:33b, MSG

Follow Jesus:

Put Jesus First!

Matthew 6:33a, MSG

Follow Jesus:

Put Jesus First!

Luke 9:23b, MSG

Follow Jesus:

Put Jesus First!

Luke 9:23a, MSG

Don't love the world's ways. Don't love the world's goods. Love of the world squeezes out love for the Father.

Practically everything that goes on in the world—wanting your own way, wanting everything for yourself, wanting to appear important—has nothing to do with the Father. It just isolates you from him.

Don't become so well-adjusted to your culture that you fit into it without even thinking. Instead, fix your attention on God. You'll be changed from the inside out.

Readily recognize what he wants from you, and quickly respond to it. Unlike the culture around you, always dragging you down to its level of immaturity, God brings the best out of you, develops well-formed maturity in you.

follow Jesus:
Be Different like Jesus!

1 John 2:16, MSG

follow Jesus:
Be Different like Jesus!

1 John 2:15, MSG

follow Jesus:
Be Different like Jesus!

Romans 12:2b, MSG

follow Jesus:
Be Different like Jesus!

Romans 12:2a, MSG

With all this going for us, my dear, dear friends, stand your ground. And don't hold back.

Throw yourselves into the work of the Master, confident that nothing you do for him is a waste of time or effort.

When you find yourselves flagging in your faith, go over that story again, item by item,

That long litany of hostility he plowed through. *That* will shoot adrenaline into your souls!

follow Jesus:
Hold Tight to Jesus!

1 Corinthians 15:58b, MSG

---

follow Jesus:
Hold Tight to Jesus!

1 Corinthians 15:58a, MSG

---

follow Jesus:
Hold Tight to Jesus!

Hebrews 12:3b, MSG

---

follow Jesus:
Hold Tight to Jesus!

Hebrews 12:3a, MSG

That is what the Son of Man has done: He came to serve, not to be served—

And then to give away his life in exchange for many who are held hostage.

Remember, our Message is not about ourselves; we're proclaiming Jesus Christ, the Master.

All we are is messengers, errand runners from Jesus for you.

Honor God with everything you own; give him the first and the best.

Your barns will burst, your wine vats will brim over.

Remember: A stingy planter gets a stingy crop; a lavish planter gets a lavish crop. I want each of you to take plenty of time to think it over, and

Make up your own mind what you will give. That will protect you against sob stories and arm-twisting. God loves it when the giver delights in the giving.

follow Jesus:
Share!

Proverbs 3:10, MSG

follow Jesus:
Share!

Proverbs 3:9, MSG

follow Jesus:
Share!

2 Corinthians 9:7, MSG

follow Jesus:
Share!

2 Corinthians 9:6, MSG

What you'll get is the Holy Spirit. And when the Holy Spirit comes on you,

You will be able to be my witnesses in Jerusalem, all over Judea and Samaria, even to the ends of the world.

Go out and train everyone you meet, far and near, in this way of life, marking them by baptism in the threefold name: Father, Son, and Holy Spirit.

Then instruct them in the practice of all I have commanded you. I'll be with you as you do this, day after day after day, right up to the end of the age.

Follow Jesus:

Love the Whole World!

Acts 1:8b, MSG

Follow Jesus:

Love the Whole World!

Acts 1:8a, MSG

Follow Jesus:

Love the Whole World!

Matthew 28:20, MSG

Follow Jesus:

Love the Whole World!

Matthew 28:19, MSG

Let me give you a new command: Love one another. In the same way I loved you, you love one another.

This is how everyone will recognize that you are my disciples—when they see the love you have for each other.

My dear children, let's not just talk about love;

Let's practice real love.

Live like Jesus:
Love!

John 13:35, MSG

Live like Jesus:
Love!

John 13:34, MSG

Live like Jesus:
Love!

1 John 3:18b, MSG

Live like Jesus:
Love!

1 John 3:18a, MSG

Don't push your way to the front; don't sweet-talk your way to the top. Put yourself aside, and help others get ahead.

Don't be obsessed with getting your own advantage. Forget yourselves long enough to lend a helping hand.

And you who are younger must follow your leaders. But all of you, leaders and followers alike, are to be down to earth with each other, for—
God has had it with the proud,

But takes delight in just plain people. So be content with who you are, and don't put on airs. God's strong hand is on you; he'll promote you at the right time.

Live like Jesus:

Be Humble!

Philippians 2:4, MSG

Live like Jesus:

Be Humble!

Philippians 2:3, MSG

Live like Jesus:

Be Humble!

1 Peter 5:6, MSG

Live like Jesus:

Be Humble!

1 Peter 5:5, MSG

All of us who look forward to his Coming stay ready,

With the glistening purity of Jesus' life as a model for our own.

Friends, this world is not your home, so don't make yourselves cozy in it.

Don't indulge your ego at the expense of your soul.

Live like Jesus:
Be Pure!

1 John 3:3b, MSG

Live like Jesus:
Be Pure!

1 John 3:3a, MSG

Live like Jesus:
Be Pure!

1 Peter 2:11b, MSG

Live like Jesus:
Be Pure!

1 Peter 2:11a, MSG

Don't steal.
Don't lie.

Don't deceive
anyone.

Believe me, I do my
level best to keep a
clear conscience

Before God and
my neighbors in
everything I do.

Live like Jesus:
Tell the Truth!

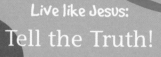

Leviticus 19:11b, MSG

Live like Jesus:
Tell the Truth!

Leviticus 19:11a, MSG

Live like Jesus:
Tell the Truth!

Acts 24:16b, MSG

Live like Jesus:
Tell the Truth!

Acts 24:16a, MSG

It's impossible to please God apart from faith. And why?

Because anyone who wants to approach God must believe both that he exists *and* that he cares enough to respond to those who seek him.

He didn't tiptoe around God's promise asking cautiously skeptical questions. He plunged into the promise and came up strong, ready for God,

Sure that God would make good on what he had said.

Live like Jesus:
Trust God!

Hebrews 11:6b, MSG

Live like Jesus:
Trust God!

Hebrews 11:6a, MSG

Live like Jesus:
Trust God!

Romans 4:21, MSG

Live like Jesus:
Trust God!

Romans 4:20, MSG

So let's not allow ourselves to get fatigued doing good. At the right time we will harvest a good crop if we don't give up, or quit.

Right now, therefore, every time we get the chance, let us work for the benefit of all, starting with the people closest to us in the community of faith.

Now that I've put you there on a hilltop, on a light stand—shine! Keep open house; be generous with your lives.

By opening up to others, you'll prompt people to open up with God, this generous Father in heaven.

Live like Jesus:
Do Your Best!

Galatians 6:10, MSG

Live like Jesus:
Do Your Best!

Galatians 6:9, MSG

Live like Jesus:
Do Your Best!

Matthew 5:16b, MSG

Live like Jesus:
Do Your Best!

Matthew 5:16a, MSG

But seek first his kingdom and his righteousness,

And all these things will be given to you as well.

Then he said to them all: "Whoever wants to be my disciple must deny themselves"

"And take up their cross daily and follow me."

Matthew 6:33b, NIV   Matthew 6:33a, NIV

Luke 9:23b, NIV   Luke 9:23a, NIV

Do not love the world or anything in the world. If anyone loves the world, love for the Father is not in them.

For everything in the world—the lust of the flesh, the lust of the eyes, and the pride of life—comes not from the Father but from the world.

Do not conform to the pattern of this world, but be transformed by the renewing of your mind.

Then you will be able to test and approve what God's will is—his good, pleasing and perfect will.

Follow Jesus:

Be Different like Jesus!

1 John 2:16, NIV

Follow Jesus:

Be Different like Jesus!

1 John 2:15, NIV

Follow Jesus:

Be Different like Jesus!

Romans 12:2b, NIV

Follow Jesus:

Be Different like Jesus!

Romans 12:2a, NIV

Therefore, my dear brothers and sisters, stand firm. Let nothing move you.

Always give yourselves fully to the work of the Lord, because you know that your labor in the Lord is not in vain.

Consider him who endured such opposition from sinners,

So that you will not grow weary and lose heart.

follow Jesus:
Hold Tight to Jesus!

1 Corinthians 15:58b, NIV

follow Jesus:
Hold Tight to Jesus!

1 Corinthians 15:58a, NIV

follow Jesus:
Hold Tight to Jesus!

Hebrews 12:3b, NIV

follow Jesus:
Hold Tight to Jesus!

Hebrews 12:3a, NIV

For even the Son of Man did not come to be served, but to serve,

And to give his life as a ransom for many.

For what we preach is not ourselves, but Jesus Christ as Lord,

And ourselves as your servants for Jesus' sake.

Follow Jesus: Serve Others!
Mark 10:45b, NIV

Follow Jesus: Serve Others!
Mark 10:45a, NIV

Follow Jesus: Serve Others!
2 Corinthians 4:5b, NIV

Follow Jesus: Serve Others!
2 Corinthians 4:5a, NIV

Honor the LORD with
your wealth,
with the firstfruits of
all your crops;

Then your barns
will be filled to
overflowing, and
your vats will brim
over with new wine.

Remember this:
Whoever sows
sparingly will also
reap sparingly,
and whoever sows
generously will also
reap generously.

Each of you should
give what you have
decided in your
heart to give, not
reluctantly or under
compulsion, for
God loves a cheerful
giver.

follow Jesus:
Share!
Proverbs 3:10, NIV

follow Jesus:
Share!
Proverbs 3:9, NIV

follow Jesus:
Share!
2 Corinthians 9:7, NIV

follow Jesus:
Share!
2 Corinthians 9:6, NIV

But you will receive power when the Holy Spirit comes on you;

N

And you will be my witnesses in Jerusalem, and in all Judea and Samaria, and to the ends of the earth.

N

Therefore go and make disciples of all nations, baptizing them in the name of the Father and of the Son and of the Holy Spirit,

N

And teaching them to obey everything I have commanded you. And surely I am with you always, to the very end of the age.

N

follow Jesus:
Love the Whole World!

Acts 1:8b, NIV

follow Jesus:
Love the Whole World!

Acts 1:8a, NIV

follow Jesus:
Love the Whole World!

Matthew 28:20, NIV

follow Jesus:
Love the Whole World!

Matthew 28:19, NIV

A new command I give you: Love one another. As I have loved you, so you must love one another.

By this everyone will know that you are my disciples, if you love one another.

Dear children, let us not love with words or speech

But with actions and in truth.

Live like Jesus: Love!
John 13:35, NIV

Live like Jesus: Love!
John 13:34, NIV

Live like Jesus: Love!
1 John 3:18b, NIV

Live like Jesus: Love!
1 John 3:18a, NIV

Do nothing out of selfish ambition or vain conceit. Rather, in humility value others above yourselves,

Not looking to your own interests but each of you to the interests of the others.

In the same way, you who are younger, submit yourselves to your elders. All of you, clothe yourselves with humility toward one another, because, "God opposes the proud

But shows favor to the humble." Humble yourselves, therefore, under God's mighty hand, that he may lift you up in due time.

Live like Jesus:
Be Humble!

Philippians 2:4, NIV

Live like Jesus:
Be Humble!

Philippians 2:3, NIV

Live like Jesus:
Be Humble!

1 Peter 5:6, NIV

Live like Jesus:
Be Humble!

1 Peter 5:5, NIV

All who have this hope in him

Purify themselves, just as he is pure.

Dear friends, I urge you, as foreigners and exiles,

To abstain from sinful desires, which wage war against your soul.

Live like Jesus:
Be Pure!

1 John 3:3b, NIV

Live like Jesus:
Be Pure!

1 John 3:3a, NIV

Live like Jesus:
Be Pure!

1 Peter 2:11b, NIV

Live like Jesus:
Be Pure!

1 Peter 2:11a, NIV

Do not steal.
Do not lie.

Do not deceive one
another.

So I strive always to
keep my conscience

Clear before God
and man.

Live like Jesus:
Tell the Truth!

Leviticus 19:11b, NIV

Live like Jesus:
Tell the Truth!

Leviticus 19:11a, NIV

Live like Jesus:
Tell the Truth!

Acts 24:16b, NIV

Live like Jesus:
Tell the Truth!

Acts 24:16a, NIV

And without faith it is impossible to please God,

Because anyone who comes to him must believe that he exists and that he rewards those who earnestly seek him.

Yet he did not waver through unbelief regarding the promise of God, but was strengthened in his faith and gave glory to God,

Being fully persuaded that God had power to do what he had promised.

Live like Jesus:
Trust God!

Hebrews 11:6b, NIV

Live like Jesus:
Trust God!

Hebrews 11:6a, NIV

Live like Jesus:
Trust God!

Romans 4:21, NIV

Live like Jesus:
Trust God!

Romans 4:20, NIV

Let us not become weary in doing good, for at the proper time we will reap a harvest if we do not give up.

Therefore, as we have opportunity, let us do good to all people, especially to those who belong to the family of believers.

In the same way, let your light shine before others,

That they may see your good deeds and glorify your Father in heaven.

Live like Jesus:
Do Your Best!

Galatians 6:10, NIV

Live like Jesus:
Do Your Best!

Galatians 6:9, NIV

Live like Jesus:
Do Your Best!

Matthew 5:16b, NIV

Live like Jesus:
Do Your Best!

Matthew 5:16a, NIV